W9-AWY-790

SNAKES

Hognose Snakes

by Adele D. Richardson

Consultants:
The staff of Black Hills Reptile Gardens
Rapid City, South Dakota

CAPSTONE
HIGH-INTEREST
BOOKS

an imprint of Capstone Press
Mankato, Minnesota

Capstone High-Interest Books are published by Capstone Press
151 Good Counsel Drive, P.O. Box 669, Mankato, Minnesota 56002
http://www.capstone-press.com

Library of Congress Cataloging-in-Publication Data
Richardson, Adele, 1966–
    Hognose snakes / by Adele D. Richardson.
    p. cm.—(Snakes)
    Summary: Describes the physical features, habitat, hunting, and mating
methods of hognose snakes.
    Includes bibliographical references (p. 45) and index.
    ISBN 0-7368-2136-8 (hardcover)
    1. Hognose snakes—Juvenile literature. [1. Hognose snakes. 2. Snakes.] I. Title.
II. Series: Snakes (Mankato, Minn.)
QL666.O636 R53 2004
597.96′2—dc21
                                         2002155928

Editorial Credits
Tom Adamson, editor; Patrick Dentinger, book designer; Jo Miller, photo researcher

Photo Credits
Cover: Mexican hognose snake, Visuals Unlimited/G and C Merker

Bruce Coleman Inc./Joe McDonald, 6, 11; Bob Gossington, 30; Jack Dermid, 32
James E. Gerholdt, 8, 15, 18–19, 20, 27
Joe McDonald, 22, 24, 34, 39
Unicorn Stock Photos/Russell R. Grungke, 44
Visuals Unlimited/Gilbert L. Twiest, 12; Dale R. Jackson, 16; Joe McDonald, 29;
    Rob & Ann Simpson, 36; G and C Merker, 40

1 2 3 4 5 6 08 07 06 05 04 03

Table of Contents

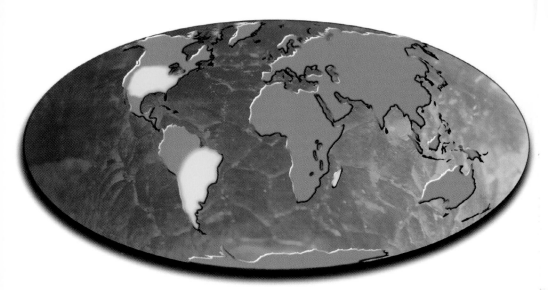

Yellow represents areas where hognose snakes live.

Fast Facts about Hognose Snakes

Scientific Names: North American hognose snakes are members of the Colubridae family. They belong to the genus *Heterodon*.

Size: Hognose snakes are between 1 and 5 feet (31 and 152 centimeters) long.

Range: Hognose snakes live in North America, South America, and Madagascar.

Description:	Hognose snakes have pointed snouts that turn up at the end. Most hognoses are yellow, light brown, orange, or gray with dark blotches.
Habitat:	Hognose snakes live in areas with dry, sandy soil. They burrow into the dry ground for protection or to find food.
Food:	Hognose snakes eat mostly frogs and toads. They also eat rodents, lizards, turtles, and reptile eggs.
Habits:	When threatened, hognose snakes flatten their head and neck. They hiss loudly, but they rarely bite. If a predator does not leave, hognoses roll onto their back and play dead.
Reproduction:	Hognose snakes mate during spring. About one month later, the females lay between four and 60 eggs. The eggs hatch in about eight weeks. The young take care of themselves.

CHAPTER 1

Hognose Snakes

Hognose snakes are well known for playing dead when threatened. A hognose rolls onto its back with its mouth open and tongue hanging out. A hognose may even spit up blood and give off a bad odor to make the act seem real. If turned onto its stomach, the hognose quickly rolls back over.

Colubridae Family

All snakes are reptiles. Turtles, lizards, and alligators are also reptiles. These animals are cold-blooded. Their body temperature changes with their surroundings. About 2,400 species of snakes live in the world.

Hognose snakes have a turned-up snout.

South American hognoses are brightly colored.

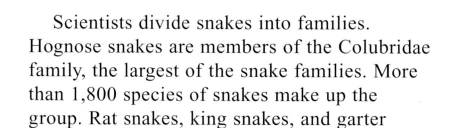

Scientists divide snakes into families. Hognose snakes are members of the Colubridae family, the largest of the snake families. More than 1,800 species of snakes make up the group. Rat snakes, king snakes, and garter snakes are also members of Colubridae.

Most Colubridae snakes are nonvenomous. Venomous snakes inject a poisonous liquid called venom into prey when they bite. Only a few colubrids are venomous. Their venom is rarely deadly to people.

Hognose Snake Genera

Each snake family is divided into genera. All snakes in a genus are closely related. The hognose snake genera are *Heterodon, Lystrophis,* and *Leioheterodon.*

Hognose snakes in North America belong to the *Heterodon* genus. This genus has three species. *Heterodon* means "different tooth." These snakes have larger back teeth than other colubrids.

South American hognose snakes belong to the genus *Lystrophis.* Six species make up this group. Snakes of *Lystrophis* have thick bodies and turned-up noses like the *Heterodon* snakes. But South American hognoses have bright bands of color. They look like the venomous coral snakes that live in the same area. They are sometimes called "false corals."

Another genus of hognose snake is named *Leioheterodon*. These snakes are known as Madagascan hognose snakes. The Madagascan hognoses are large and strong. They live only in dry, forested areas of Madagascar. This island lies off the eastern coast of Africa.

Madagascan hognoses are black with yellow markings.

CHAPTER 2

Hognose Species

Hognoses in North America are named for the part of the continent they live in. One species, the western hognose, has three subspecies.

Eastern Hognose Snake

The scientific name for the eastern hognose snake is *Heterodon platyrhinos*. Scientists named this species for a flattened scale on the tip of its nose. Platyrhinos means flat nose.

The eastern hognose is the largest snake in the *Heterodon* genus. Like other hognoses, these snakes have heavy, stout bodies. The adults grow to between 20 and 34 inches

The eastern hognose has a flat scale on top of its snout.

(51 and 86 centimeters) long. Females are usually a little bigger than the males.

Eastern hognoses can have a variety of colors. The scales on their back can be yellow, brown, gray, red, orange, or black. Many eastern hognoses have dark brown or black blotches. The blotches form patterns. Some eastern hognoses are all black or gray.

The underbelly color of the eastern hognose also varies. Some may have yellow, light gray, or pink scales. Others may have a dark underbelly. Usually, blotches of gray or green mark the snakes' underbellies.

Western Hognose Snake

Western hognoses' snouts are more curved than eastern hognoses' snouts. Most western hognoses grow to between 16 and 25 inches (41 and 64 centimeters). But some can reach 36 inches (91 centimeters) long.

Western hognoses are light brown, gray, or yellow. They have dark brown or black blotches running down their back. On their sides are two rows of smaller spots. Western hognoses have black scales under their tail.

The turned-up snout is more noticeable in the western hognose species, including this plains hognose.

Western Hognose Snake Subspecies

The three western hognose subspecies are similar. Snakes are placed in subspecies because of differences in color, markings, or size.

The three subspecies have small physical differences. The dusty hognose looks like it is covered in dust. It has fewer blotches on its body than other western hognoses. The plains hognose has more blotches than the dusty hognose. The Mexican hognose has fewer

The southern hognose is the smallest of the North American hognose snakes.

scales between and behind its nostrils than the other hognoses. It is often more colorful than other western hognoses.

Southern Hognose Snake
The southern hognoses' snouts are also more curved than those of the eastern hognoses. Southern hognoses are the smallest of the

HOGNOSE SNAKE SPECIES

common name	scientific name
eastern hognose -	*Heterodon platyrhinos*
southern hognose -	*Heterodon simus*
western hognose -	*Heterodon nasicus*

The western hognose is divided into 3 subspecies:

dusty hognose -	*Heterodon nasicus gloydi*
Mexican hognose -	*Heterodon nasicus kennerlyi*
plains hognose -	*Heterodon nasicus nasicus*

Heterodon genus. They can be between 12 and 21 inches (31 and 53 centimeters) long.

Southern hognoses look much like western hognose snakes. Their scales can be yellow, gray, or light brown. They have brown, black, or dark gray blotches on their back. A few scales often are red. Their sides have rows of smaller spots. Their underbelly is usually white or cream-colored with gray or brown blotches.

Tail

Head

Turned-up Nose

Plains Hognose

CHAPTER 3

Habitat

All the species of hognose snake live in North America, South America, or on Madagascar. Most hognoses live in areas with dry, sandy soil. They use their turned-up noses to burrow into loose dirt. They burrow to hunt for toads in the ground and to lay eggs.

North American Hognose Snakes

Eastern hognose snakes range from southeastern Canada to Florida. The snakes can be found in fields or woods with dry, sandy soil. Some eastern hognoses also live along the sandy coasts of the Atlantic Ocean and the Gulf of Mexico.

All hognoses use their snouts to burrow into loose dirt.

Mexican hognoses live in the southwestern United States and northern Mexico. Most hognoses live in areas where there is dry soil.

Western hognoses live in central North America. They are found between Arizona and Arkansas, and from southern Canada to Mexico. They prefer open areas of land with soft soil. They live in prairies and on farmland.

Some western hognoses live in the dry bottoms of mountain canyons.

Southern hognose snakes are only found in the southeastern United States. They range from North Carolina to Florida, and as far west as Mississippi. The snakes live mostly in sandy pine forests, fields, and dry river floodplains. Most southern hognoses live in areas that rarely get below 20 degrees Fahrenheit (minus 7 degrees Celsius) in winter.

Other Hognose Snakes

Like North American hognoses, South American hognoses prefer areas with sandy soil. They usually live in places with short grass.

Madagascan hognose snakes are found in short grass and sandy soil. They also live in dry, tropical forests. During times of heavy rain, the snakes are not active. They will only come out of their shelters to hunt for food when the rain stops.

CHAPTER 4

Hunting

Hognose snakes are carnivores. They hunt and eat other animals. Toads are hognoses' most common food. They will also eat frogs, lizards, small snakes, mice, and reptile eggs. Small birds that nest near the ground are sometimes prey for hognose snakes.

Senses for Hunting

Hognose snakes do not see as well as people do. Most can tell the difference between light and dark. They can also detect some nearby movement to help them find prey.

Hognose snakes do not hear as well as people do, either. They do not even have ears.

Hognose snakes eat frogs, toads, lizards, mice, and reptile eggs.

The snakes use their whole body to sense sounds. As prey or an enemy nears, hognoses feel the movement in the ground.

The ability to smell is the most important sense hognoses use for hunting. A hognose flicks out its tongue while searching for prey. The tongue collects the scents in the air. It then carries these scents to the Jacobson's organ. This organ is located on the roof of a snake's mouth. It helps the snake find prey and know what kind of animal it is.

Hunting Prey

Hognose snakes are diurnal. They are active and hunt during the day. Hognoses hunt most often in the early morning and late afternoon. At night, they stay hidden in a shelter.

Hognoses use their turned-up nose to dig for food. Toads often hide underground. Hognoses find toads by moving their head from side to side in the soil. This burrowing motion removes the sand or soil on top of the

Snakes use their tongue to smell.

prey. As soon as a toad is uncovered, a hognose quickly bites it.

Toads inhale air as a way to defend themselves. This action can make their bodies too large for a snake to swallow. Hognose snakes have fangs on the back of their upper jaws. They use these large teeth to poke holes in the toads' bodies. This lets the air out and makes the prey easier to swallow.

Hognose venom is mild. Hognoses rarely bite people. But if a person were bitten, the area might become red and irritated. It would feel like a bee sting. But to a small animal, the venom is more powerful. It calms prey during a capture. Prey that does not move around a lot is easier for the snakes to swallow.

Swallowing Prey

Hognose snakes swallow their prey whole. The snakes usually swallow prey headfirst so that it is smothered. Prey does not struggle if it goes in headfirst. Swallowing headfirst also causes the prey's legs to fold up neatly inside the snake's body.

A hognose snake can swallow prey larger than its own head. Its upper and lower jaws are connected with ligaments. This stretchy tissue allows the snake to separate its jaws. Its mouth can stretch over a large toad or rat. Strong

Hognoses use their teeth to puncture a puffed-up toad.

muscles in the snake's throat then help pull the prey into the snake's stomach.

A snake often rests after eating so its food can digest. Digestion usually takes three to four days. Less time is needed to digest small prey than large prey.

CHAPTER 5

Mating

Many hognose snakes hibernate in winter. They often rest in burrows while hibernating. They move loose soil with their snouts to make the burrows. They may also live in unused burrows made by other animals. Snakes that are hibernating lie very still. Their breathing and heartbeat slow down.

Hognose snakes wake up from hibernation in spring. The snakes then begin searching for a mate. When females are ready to mate, they give off a scent. The males follow this scent until they find a female.

A female hognose can lay up to 60 eggs at one time.

Hognoses use an egg tooth to break out of their soft, leathery eggs.

Courtship

Once a male hognose finds a female, courtship begins. During courtship, the male rubs his chin along the female's back. He often flicks his tongue along her body. Then the two snakes twist their bodies together for mating. The snakes may stay joined for a few minutes or several hours.

After mating, the male hognose spends several days trailing the female. The trailing male follows the female wherever she goes. He does this because other males will try to mate with her. The trailing male keeps other males away. After a few days of trailing, the male snake leaves. If the female is still giving off her scent, she will attract another male to mate with her.

Eggs and Young

About one month after mating, the females are ready to lay eggs. The females may dig burrows and lay the eggs inside. Sometimes they lay eggs in piles of rotting wood or leaves. Female hognoses lay between four and 60 eggs at one time. After the eggs are laid, they are left to develop without the mother's protection. The heat from the sun keeps them warm.

The outsides of hognose snake eggs are soft and leathery. They stick together. The eggs

absorb air and water. The young snakes inside need air and water.

The eggs hatch in about two months. Young hognoses use an egg tooth to cut an opening in the leathery shells. An egg tooth is a tiny thorn-like spur on a young snake's upper jaw. It falls off soon after hatching. The young can take several hours, or even days, before they completely leave the eggs.

The newly hatched young are usually between 5 and 10 inches (13 and 25 centimeters) long. They look much like the adult hognoses. The young snakes are on their own as soon as they hatch. They must find their own food and shelter. They eat insects and young frogs and toads.

A hognose might take several hours to leave its egg.

CHAPTER 6

Hognose Snakes and People

A common myth about hognose snakes is that they have poisonous breath. The myth says that hognoses mix poison with their breath and then breathe at people. But hognose snakes cause little harm to people. This myth started because of a hognose's behavior when defending itself.

A hognose snake puts on a big show when it feels threatened. It flattens its head and neck to make a hood. This behavior makes it look like a deadly cobra, a snake famous for its large hood. The snake then hisses loudly

Hognoses flatten their head and neck when they feel threatened.

and strikes. A hognose does not bite when it strikes. Usually, its mouth is closed.

Playing Dead

If the snake still feels threatened after striking, it plays dead. A hognose puts a lot of effort into playing dead. A hognose rolls onto its back and twitches, pretending to be in great pain. The snake's mouth opens and its tongue hangs out. Sometimes a hognose spits up blood or undigested food. It may also give off a bad odor. Some predators will not eat a dead animal that smells bad.

If flipped onto its stomach, the hognose quickly rolls back over. The snake will stay in this position until the danger has passed.

The hognose's behavior has earned it some nicknames. It is also known as a spreading adder, false cobra, puff adder, and death adder.

Hognose Snakes as Pets

Some people keep hognose snakes as pets. Hognoses are not aggressive. They rarely bite their keepers. Western hognoses are believed

Hognoses play dead as a defensive strategy.

to be easier to tame and to handle than the other species.

   People should learn all they can about hognoses before deciding to keep one as a pet. Like any other pet, snakes need care. They need proper food and a clean place to live. It can be difficult to find the toads that hognoses

Hognoses eat rodents that are a nuisance to people.

usually eat. Pet hognoses can become sick. They must be taken to a veterinarian, just like any other pet.

Benefits and Conservation

Hognose snakes can benefit people. They keep toad and frog populations from getting too big.

They also help control rodent populations. Mice can eat farmers' crops and spread diseases. By eating these animals, hognoses help prevent the spread of some diseases.

In some parts of North America, the hognose population is shrinking. Fewer of these snakes live in the wild because their habitats have been destroyed. Many snake habitats are ruined when people build roads or houses. Hognoses have also been killed because of their defensive behavior. They seem like a deadly snake when they flatten their necks and hiss.

Hognoses are on Canada's protected species list. It is illegal to hunt or hurt hognoses in Canada. Some places in the United States also protect these snakes. In Massachusetts, it is illegal to kill or capture hognoses. The southern hognose may soon be considered an endangered species.

Words to Know

adder (AD-ur)—a venomous snake from Europe; adders belong to the family Viperidae.

burrow (BUR-oh)—to dig a hole; a burrow can also be a hole in the ground that an animal makes.

carnivore (KAR-nuh-vor)—an animal that hunts and eats other animals

cobra (KOH-bruh)—a large, venomous snake that spreads its skin so that its head and neck look like a hood; cobras live in Asia and Africa.

digest (dye-JEST)—to break down food so it can be used by the body

diurnal (dye-UR-nuhl)—active during the day

endangered species (en-DAYN-jurd SPEE-sheez)—a type of animal that is in danger of dying out

floodplain (FLUHD-plane)—an area of low land that sometimes floods during heavy rains

genus (JEE-nuhss)—a group of plants or animals that are related; genera is more than one genus.

hibernate (HYE-bur-nate)—to be inactive during winter

ligament (LIG-uh-muhnt)—a strong, stretchy band of tissue that connects bones

predator (PRED-uh-tur)—an animal that hunts other animals for food

prey (PRAY)—an animal hunted by another animal for food

species (SPEE-sheez)—a specific type of plant or animal

venom (VEN-uhm)—poison produced by some snakes

To Learn More

Behler, Deborah, and John Behler. *Snakes*. Animalways. New York: Benchmark Books, 2001.

Berger, Gilda, and Melvin Berger. *Can Snakes Crawl Backward?: Questions and Answers about Reptiles*. Scholastic Question and Answer Series. New York: Scholastic Reference, 2001.

Greenaway, Theresa. *Snakes*. The Secret World Of. Austin, Texas: Raintree Steck-Vaughn, 2001.

Mattison, Christopher. *Snake*. New York: DK Publishing, 1999.

Mudd-Ruth, Maria. *Snakes*. Animals, Animals. New York: Marshall Cavendish, 2002.

Useful Addresses

Arizona Herpetological Association
P.O. Box 64531
Phoenix, AZ 85082-4531

Black Hills Reptile Gardens
P.O. Box 620
Rapid City, SD 57709

The Minnesota Herpetological Society
The Bell Museum of Natural History
10 Church Street SE
Minneapolis, MN 55455-0104

The Ontario Herpetological Society
P.O. Box 244
Stn Port Credit
Mississauga, ON L5G 4L8
Canada

Internet Sites

Do you want to learn more about hognoses and other snakes?
Visit the FactHound at *http://www.facthound.com*

FactHound can track down many sites to help you. All the FactHound sites are hand-selected by our editors. FactHound will fetch the best, most accurate information to answer your questions.

IT'S EASY! IT'S FUN!
1) Go to *http://www.facthound.com*
2) Type in: 0736821368
3) Click on "FETCH IT" and FactHound will put you on the trail of several helpful links.

You can also search by subject or book title. So, relax and let our pal FactHound do the research for you!

Index